T0017448

SURFING AND WINDSURFING

J. Poolos

rosen publishing's
rosen central®

NEW YORK

Published in 2016 by The Rosen Publishing Group, Inc.
29 East 21st Street, New York, NY 10010

Copyright © 2016 by The Rosen Publishing Group, Inc.

First Edition

Library of Congress Cataloging-in-Publication Data

Poolos, Jamie.
Surfing and windsurfing/J. Poolos.
        pages cm.—(Sports to the extreme)
Includes bibliographical references and index.
ISBN 978-1-4994-3573-3 (library bound) — ISBN 978-1-4994-3575-7 (pbk.) —
ISBN 978-1-4994-3576-4 (6-pack)
1. Surfing—Juvenile literature. 2. Windsurfing—Juvenile literature. 3. Extreme sports—Juvenile literature. I. Title.
GV839.55.P66 2016
797.3'2—dc23

2014046168

Manufactured in the United States of America

CONTENTS

INTRODUCTION

We have all seen surfers crouched on their boards, flying through the "tube" of a big wave like nothing can stop them. They seem to defy gravity, gaining speed and somehow staying just ahead of the breaking wave that comes crashing down behind them. They make us wonder, how cool would it be to surf?

Surfing is one of the most popular and exciting water sports in the world. It has a rich and interesting history dating back to at least the eighteenth century. It is done in some of the most exotic places around. Surfing has a huge following. The International Surfing Association estimates there are more than 23 million surfers worldwide. People of all ages enjoy the sport as a fun, exciting activity. Thrill seekers try to outlast one another on the sea's biggest waves. And the best surfers travel the globe to compete in high-stakes contests.

But surfing can be dangerous. Each year, the surfing community loses a few of its members. Some are knocked unconscious and drown. Others are swept out to sea. And even a few die of shark attacks. For surfers, it's "safety first" and live to surf another day.

There is another sport that has a lot in common with surfing. Windsurfing is a competitive sport for action seekers who love speed.

A surfer rides a tube, or barrel, with perfect form. In order to slow his speed so he can stay in the barrel longer, he drags his inside hand on the face of the wave.

Windsurfing is a combination of surfing and sailing. Windsurfers ride modified surfboards that are powered by the wind. In the 1980s, windsurfing was one of the most popular activities around. People seeking sun and fun turned to the new sport in large numbers, creating an explosion of windsurfers on the world's beaches.

Both sports are high-risk, high-reward activities. That's why surfers and windsurfers treat the oceans with respect and put safety before fun. If you think riding the waves on beautiful beaches is for you, suit up, grab your board, and give surfing or windsurfing a try. These extreme sports will take your breath away!

CHAPTER ONE

THE HISTORIES OF SURFING AND WINDSURFING

The histories of surfing and windsurfing could not be more different. Surfing is an ancient tradition that began hundreds of years ago in the tropical islands of the Pacific. In contrast, windsurfing began only in the twentieth century. Yet both are very popular action sports.

THE HISTORY OF SURFING

It's not easy to tell exactly when a sport as old as surfing began. It is believed that as long ago as 1500 BCE, fishermen in the Pacific Ocean rode the waves in outrigger canoes. They used the waves to carry them over coral reefs when they returned to land with the day's catch. These men, the first "surfers," were true watermen. They were strong swimmers who were skilled at handling canoes in giant surf. They were experts at reading the ocean's dangerous currents and tides, and they were great divers and spear fisher-men. Surfing was born of their work. Somewhere along the way, people realized surfing was fun, and it became a form of play.

The first recorded instance of surfing occurred in 1778, more than 230 years ago. That happened when the British explorer

In the 1800s, surfing was a social activity with great spiritual meaning for Hawaiians.

Captain James Cook witnessed natives riding boards on the waves in Hawaii. It was the first record of a European encounter with Hawaii. But surfing probably began long before that in the Polynesian Islands. There are surfing songs and chants that tell of surfing more than five hundred years ago.

In Hawaii, surfing (or *he'e nalu*) was a sport only for the upper class. Surfers said prayers and designed special surfboards as offerings to the gods. In fact, surfing was considered a sacred act. Surfing thrived in the native culture until the early 1900s. As more Europeans traveled to the islands to explore and settle, they brought diseases that made the natives sick. As the native population dwindled, there were fewer natives to practice the tradition of surfing. Just as surfing was about to become extinct, along came its saviors.

Slowly, more and more tourists began to take up the sport. Descriptions of surfing were spreading to other parts of the world. This was in large part due to the efforts of men like George Freeth. In 1907, the Hawaiian native demonstrated surfing in Redondo Beach, California. After the demonstration, Freeth stayed in California. Within a few years, people were surfing in other areas of Southern California.

Meanwhile, a surfing legend in the making was about to bring the sport to the other side of the globe. Duke Kahanamoku was a strong swimmer who had won six Olympic medals. But he was also known as the father of modern surfing. It was Kahanamoku who helped make surfing popular in Hawaii again. The expert waterman also introduced surfing to Australia and New Zealand, places where the sport remains popular today.

As surfing was slowly taking off on the West Coast of the United States,

This statue of the famous surfer Duke Kahanamoku stands at Waikiki Beach, Honolulu, Hawaii. Born in 1890, Kahanamoku was surfing's greatest promoter.

MODERN SURFING'S GREATEST AMBASSADOR

If there is one surfing legend of modern times that surfing knows and loves, it's Duke Kahanamoku. Born in 1890 in Honolulu, Hawaii, Kahanamoku was a skilled waterman who excelled at swimming, paddling, and surfing. As a swimmer, he set world records and won multiple Olympic gold medals. In what was described as a superhuman act, he once saved eight fishermen from rough waters when their boat capsized off Newport Beach, California.

As a surfer, Kahanamoku was in a league of his own. While most surfers rode waves on 6-foot (1.8-meter) boards, he used a 10-foot (3-m) board and paddled farther offshore in search of the big waves that offered longer rides. His style was graceful and elegant, more like the style of traditional surfers. But what set Kahanamoku apart from other surfers was the way he promoted surfing.

In 1912 he introduced surfing to the East Coast of the United States, when he gave a demonstration in Atlantic City, New Jersey. In the following years, his exhibitions of the Hawaiian style of surfing in Australia and New Zealand attracted thousands of viewers. He is also credited with making surfing popular in Southern California during this time.

Kahanamoku died in 1968. He was surfing's greatest ambassador and an inspiration to the generations of surfers and innovators who followed.

surfboards began to change. In the old days, a surfer hiked through a rain forest in search of a suitable redwood tree from which to carve a board. Then the kahuna, or board shaper, said a prayer to the gods, thanking them for the gift, and cut down the tree. Once the tree was dragged home, the kahuna shaped a long, heavy board. These boards weighed upward of 175 pounds (79 kg). In the early 1930s, board shapers like Tom Blake ushered in the popularity of smaller, hollow boards that weighed only 100 pounds (45 kg). Soon, boards like Blake's famous cigar-shaped hollow board would weigh a mere 60 pounds (27 kg). The smaller boards were not as stable in big waves, but they were much easier to maneuver, and they quickly became popular with surfers.

A CULTURE DEVELOPS

By the 1940s, surfing was not a mainstream activity. But it was popular enough to have its own culture. The California surfers of this time were known for being tough and daring thrill seekers. Their lifestyle revolved around the waves and the weather. They also developed a language and music of their own. They were rugged people who didn't feel like they fit in with mainstream society and were looking for something different from life.

Surfers would pack into station wagons and vans, their boards strapped to the roofs, and head out on "surfing safaris." They surfed up and down the California coast, camping on the beaches and eating whatever they could lay their hands on. They were living the life many young people wanted to live. But for most young people, it wasn't practical to give up school or a job just to surf.

Gradually, more and more people found out about surfing and gave it a try. Soon the population of weekend surfers exploded. As the fad caught on, surfing became a part of mainstream culture. Surf music, featuring a unique guitar style, was played on the popular radio stations. By the 1960s, bands like the Beach Boys painted sonic seascapes of the surfing life and the California culture. Hollywood made movies about the beach culture with big name stars like Frankie Avalon and Elvis Presley. Before long, everyone in the country knew about the sport.

Since then, surfing has grown into a mainstream pastime all over the world. The surfing culture remains strong, and it has kept up with the changing times. Recent innovations like portable, waterproof

By the early 1960s, surf culture had taken hold in America. Movies like *Blue Hawaii*, starring Elvis Presley, depicted the surfing lifestyle.

LEGENDARY SURF MOVIES

By the end of the 1950s, surfing was popular even among people who had never seen the ocean. One reason was the glut of movies that brought the surfing culture into movie theaters all over the country. First came *Gidget*, the 1959 teen movie about a surfer girl. This was followed by *Gidget Goes Hawaiian* and the 1961 hit *Blue Hawaii*, starring rock 'n' roll's Elvis Presley. By 1963, the genre focused more on the culture and less on surfing, with *Beach Party*, starring Frankie Avalon and Annette Funicello. Studios began to copy the beach party formula, and the theaters were flooded with movies about teenage exploits on the beach.

But not all surf movies were fictional accounts of beachgoers. In 1966, an unknown filmmaker named Bruce Brown made what surfing purists at the time called the best surfing movie ever made. *The Endless Summer* followed two surfers and their surfing friends around the world. It showed them surfing in Australia, Tahiti, and Hawaii, among other locations. The film was highly acclaimed for its beautiful cinematic photography and its casual, sometimes cleverly humorous tone. It showed intelligent, resourceful young men who in their search for the perfect wave valued unique experiences in nature over college and the security of a career—an attitude that was consistent with the ideals of 1960s youth.

cameras and high-definition cameras have enabled videographers to capture the best surfing footage. This allows even nonsurfers to feel like they're surfing from the comfort of their own homes. People of all ages still tune in to surf reports, drive to the beach, and squeeze into their wet suits. They paddle out past the "break" and wait for the perfect wave.

THE HISTORY OF WINDSURFING

Windsurfing began in 1948 when Newman Darby attached a sail to a board and sailed it around a lake in Pennsylvania. Nearly twenty years later, an engineer named Jim Drake and his neighbor Hoyle Schweitzer built a similar device and patented it. They tried out several names, including the "skate" and the "Baja board" before settling on "windsurfer." Windsurfing grew quickly. By the late 1970s, the sport was very popular all over the world. According to www.windsurfing-guide.com, one out of every three households in Europe at that time had a windsurfer.

In 1984, windsurfing was introduced to the Olympic Games. That year, Dutch windsurfer Stephan van den Berg won the event's gold medal. By the 1992 Olympic Games in Barcelona, Spain, women's windsurfing was an official Olympic sport. The first gold medal in the event was won by Barbara Kendall of New Zealand. After its rapid growth in the 1970s and 1980s, windsurfing was at the peak of

In the 1980s the popularity of windsurfing competitions soared. Here, Stephan van den Berg of the Netherlands glides to a gold medal at the 1984 Summer Olympics Games in Los Angeles.

its popularity. People of all ages were attracted to the speed and thrills windsurfing offered.

But by the mid-1990s, it began a rapid decline. There were several reasons for this. Equipment became more specialized and expensive. Because the companies that built windsurfers focused on developing newer and faster rigs, they neglected the easy-to-use equipment that beginners needed. As a result, fewer people took up the sport. Today, windsurfing is gaining momentum once again, as beginner equipment is easily found, and more young people are learning the fundamentals of surfing and sailing.

CHAPTER TWO

SURFING AND WIND-SURFING TODAY

Today's surfers ride the same waves as their surfing forefathers did, but many aspects of the sport and its culture have changed. The same can be said for windsurfing, which is making a comeback after a decline in popularity.

MODERN SURFING

Surfing is a very popular extreme sport today, and it is important to sports culture in America and worldwide. There are more people surfing today than ever. There are weekend surfers and everyday surfers. In coastal areas like California and Hawaii, businessmen head to the beaches before work to catch some waves. When school is out, students can be found in the lineup just off shore, waiting to catch their waves. It's obvious that surfing is a huge part of many peoples' lives.

Now more than ever, the sport of surfing and the culture that surrounds it are organized. One way that this is evident is in the number of regional and international contests that gather the world's top surfers to see who is best. Advanced surfers who want to compete under a set of rules are drawn to these

15

Surfing competitions draw the world's most competitive surfers, along with big crowds and big prize money. Some surfers compete on a world tour that visits the best surfing spots in exotic locations all over the world.

Sunset Beach
North Shore, Oahu Hawai'i

FINAL

DUSTY PAYNE
HAWAII

IAN WALSH
HAWAII

MICHEL BOUREZ
TAHITI

SEBASTIAN ZIETZ
HAWAII

competitions. The Association of Surfing Professionals (ASP) is the governing body for professional surfers. It crowns surfing's world champions every year over a series of events. Recently, the tour included ten events in exotic locations like Tahiti, Fiji, and Rio.

In surf competitions, judges score surfers on their technique and expression. Usually the surfer who rides a wave with the most speed, control, and power gets the highest score. Big competitions draw hundreds of the world's best surfers and thousands of spectators. The format varies from competition to competition. In most events, however, surfers are grouped in heats, with the top scorers in each heat advancing to a semifinal. The top scorers of the semifinal reach the final round, where the champion is determined.

BIG WAVE SURFING

One type of competition that has become extremely popular is big wave surfing. With this kind of

Big wave surfing is more popular than ever. The most famous big wave competition in North America is Mavericks, in California. Here, big wave surfer Grant Washburn surfs a giant breaker.

surfing, surfers paddle out to catch waves at least 20 feet (6 m) high. It seemed only the craziest surfers would take a shot at a wave that big, but surfers craved bigger and bigger waves. The problem was that it was exhausting to paddle out far enough to catch the biggest waves and impossible to paddle fast enough to catch one.

In the early 1990s, a few surfers, including Laird Hamilton and Dave Kalama, developed a technique that enabled surfers to reach these big waves and to be able to catch them and surf them. They used jet skis and towropes to tow surfers out to deep water. Sometimes they even place the surfers into the wave. Once the surfer is in the wave and on the move, he lets go of the towrope, and the jet ski powers away out of danger. This new technique enabled big wave surfers to break the 30-foot (9-m) barrier. (That is the height of a three-story building.) Today, some surfers are able to surf waves 50 feet (15 m) high.

While big wave surfing is spectacular, it is also very dangerous. Surfers can be pounded into sharp reefs and held underwater for more than a minute. More than a few experienced big wave surfers have died in the surf over the past five years. Only surfers with years of experience, who are strong swimmers and superb athletes, should attempt to surf big waves. The consequences of even a small mistake can be fatal.

Mavericks is probably the most famous big wave competition. After a winter storm, when the conditions are right, waves can reach a height of 80 feet (24 m). But there are big waves all over the world. The Big Wave World Tour, a contest that spans the globe from August through February, makes stops in such exotic locales as Punta de Lobos, Chile; Punta Galea, in Basque Country; and Dungeons, South Africa. The world's bravest surfers risk life and limb to score big points and earn big money.

BIG WAVES' MOST WICKED EVENT

What event has the most enormous, gnarliest waves to surf? Mavericks. Every year, a few handfuls of the world's bravest surfers are invited to compete. The event takes place 2 miles (3.21 kilometers) offshore the coast of Northern California, near Pillar Point Harbor, and it's one of the wildest, most exciting surf contests around.

Mavericks got its name in 1967, when three locals paddled out to surf the enormous waves. The dog

Mavericks draws the world's best surfers.

belonging to one of the local's roommates joined them. His name was Maverick, and since then the waves have been known by his name. In 1975, a few local surfers braved the dangers to surf Mavericks, but the waves remained a myth to most surfers, who didn't believe they were real. By the early 1990s, more surfers gave Mavericks a try. The first contest was held in 1999 and has taken place yearly since then.

Contestants wait on standby, sometimes for weeks, for news of the perfect weather conditions that will produce giant waves. When the call comes, they have forty-eight hours to get to the site, where they are towed into the waves by jet skis. Judges watch from shore. The surfer who has the best ride takes home the $12,000 first prize and bragging rights as the gnarliest big wave surfer of the year.

A BIG BUSINESS

Over the years, surfing has evolved into a big-money business. The top pro surfers in the world earn hundreds of thousands of dollars in prize money for their efforts. The winner of a round earns about $40,000. While the best professional surfers earn a lot of prize money, they earn even more money through sponsorship. Elite surfers can be granted multiyear contracts worth millions of dollars from companies that supply surfing equipment, clothing, and accessories. Some of the big names in surfing sponsorship are Billabong, Quicksilver, Vans, and O'Neill. One of pro surfing's top earners, eleven-time ASP World Champion Kelly Slater, earned an additional $2 million over five years as Quicksilver's sponsored surfer. Most sponsorships involve less cash. It's more typical for a surfer to earn $20,000 to $50,000 for a multiyear contract.

Today, surfing is promoted with modern media like films, websites, and magazines. Low cost personal video cameras and video websites like YouTube and Vimeo have spurred a revolution in amateur surfing "movies" that anyone can access from home. The surfing industry generates approximately $7 billion every year.

Highly skilled windsurfers use waves as jumps and their sails as wings, flying high above the water, where they do flips and other tricks.

WINDSURFING TODAY

Windsurfing is certainly not as popular as it once was. A telltale sign is that windsurfing will be replaced by kitesurfing in the 2016 Olympics. Still, windsurfing maintains a world championship, regulated by the International Windsurfing Association, with stops all over the world. In North and South America, the American Windsurfing Association holds the American Windsurfing Tour each year, with events up and down both coasts and in Hawaii.

Windsurfers compete in any of several events, most of which resemble sailing races. The various classes account for different wind conditions: some classes are for high winds, and others are for moderate or light winds. But the freestyle event is different. In freestyle, windsurfers use waves as ramps. Once airborne, they perform tricks. Judges rate these tricks to determine a winner of the contest. Often these aerial moves are combined with wave rides, which are judged the same way like surfing contests are judged. Some tricks involve getting big air, and some can be done with little or no waves. Some of the most amazing tries are the backward loop and the double frontie, both of which involve high-flying, spinning moves.

Windsurfing's best-known superstar is Robby Naish. Naish proved to be a remarkable athlete even at a young age. He took up windsurfing at age eleven, and he won his first world championship in 1976 at age thirteen. Since then, he has won multiple world titles as both an amateur and professional competitor.

In the 2012 Summer Olympics in London, Dorian van Rijsselberghe of the Netherlands won the gold in the RX:X sailboarding class. (Sailboarding is another name for windsurfing.) He beat a field of thirty-eight racers, each representing a different country.

CHAPTER THREE

SURFING AND WINDSURFING EQUIPMENT

Like many extreme sports, surfing requires the right equipment for the right situation. Surfers choose their gear for safety and performance. Thanks to a healthy surfing industry, there are plenty of choices for gear that suit a variety of conditions and purposes. From beginners to experts, in warm water and cold, surfers can easily get the best gear for their needs.

SURFBOARDS

Today, surfboards are designed and crafted for a variety of purposes. Surfboards come in different sizes, shapes, and materials. Some have one fin on the bottom to help the surfer turn. Others have two or even three fins to make sharp turns or "cutbacks" easier. While manufactured boards, or "popouts," are a great choice for beginners and intermediate surfers, most experienced surfers have hand-made boards designed specifically for their weight and style.

One thing almost all modern, hand-made surfboards have in common is that they are made with a core of buoyant (floatable) foam surrounded by a hard shell. Most boards are made one at

Surfboards start as liquid that is poured into a mold to harden. They are then cut, strengthened, and glued back together. Finally, they are shaped by hand, painted, and sealed.

a time. The board maker starts by pouring a liquid mixture into a mold in the shape of the kind of surfboard that is being made. The mixture hardens into a lightweight foam, sort of like styrofoam. This is called a blank. The board maker then cuts the blank in half lengthwise and glues in a rigid piece of material called a stringer. This helps to keep the board from breaking under the stress of surfing.

The board maker then puts the blank onto a table or a pair of saw horses and traces the shape of the board he wants to care. He uses a saber saw to cut out the board. Then he uses a power planer to shape the bottom and the top of the board. Because this is all done by hand, with no machines, the board maker relies on his skill and talent to carve the perfect board.

Next comes the "glassing," the process used to make the board's hard shell. After the board is cut, it is sanded smooth. Then the board maker applies fiberglass cloth and resin, which makes the fiberglass stick to the board. When the resin hardens, the board is sanded, and another layer of fiberglass and resin is applied. This is followed by another round of sanding. Then any decals and designs are added to the board before a final coat of clear resin is applied. As a last step, the board maker wet-sands the board with fine sand paper to make the last coat of resin shine.

CHOOSING A BOARD

An experienced surfer has more than one board. On any given day, he selects the board he'll use based on the kind of surfing he wants to do. But what considerations does he weigh when choosing a board? First, there is the type of surfing he wants to do. Basically, there are three kinds of surfing: cruising, ripping, and big wave surfing.

Cruising is a more relaxed kind of surfing, where the surfer makes gradual turns. Longboards, or Malibus, are great for cruising because they are stable in the water and make smooth turns. A thruster, or shortboard, is perfect for ripping. Surfers

Surfboards come in many sizes and shapes. Experienced surfers have several boards and choose the best one for the day's conditions.

can make quick turns and do high-flying tricks with thrusters. But because thrusters are shorter and thinner, they are more difficult to ride. A "fish" is another board shape that is excellent for ripping. It's even shorter and wider than a thruster.

Big wave surfers use "guns" to surf the 30-foot (9-m) faces of those giant waves. Guns are about the same length as longboards, but the shape is different, making for easy drops on big waves. Finally, the stand-up paddleboard, or SUP, is great for carving small waves with the aid of a paddle for steering. A "foamie" is a lightweight board used only for beginners.

Surfers also need to consider the size and shape of the waves they'll be encountering. When the water is flat, the SUP is really the only choice. You can still get a great workout even without waves. With small, rolling waves, the longboard is the board of choice. Steep waves of medium height call for a fish or shortboard. These waves are great for tube riding and tricks off the lip of the wave. And of course big wave surfers know to use a gun.

BOARD TYPES IN A NUTSHELL

Longboard: Otherwise known as a Malibu, the longboard tapers toward the rear. These are great for cruising small, rolling waves.

Shortboard: Known as a thruster, the shortboard is the board of choice for ripping and aerial tricks. It is wide in the middle, coming to a point at the tip.

Fish: A fish excels at ripping. It is similar in shape to a shortboard, but it is wider in the middle and shorter.

Gun: The gun is for big wave surfing. It is a narrow board that comes to a sharp point at the tip.

Stand-up paddleboard: The SUP is usually more rounded at the point. Its paddle resembles a canoe paddle.

WET SUITS

Surfers who surf in warm waters can get by with a pair of board shorts and (for women) a top. Board shorts are durable, long-cut shorts that are easy to move in. But when the water is a medium or cold temperature, surfers wear wet suits to keep warm. This allows them to stay in the water longer and to catch more waves.

A wet suit is a tight-fitting piece of clothing made of foamed neoprene, which is like a stretchy rubber. The material has tiny bubbles in it. These bubbles contain nitrogen and act as a barrier to the cold. The bubbles also add buoyancy to the surfer, making it easier for him or her to float. Wet suits come in different thicknesses. A standard wetsuit is made of neoprene that is two millimeters thick. For surfing in water below 40 degrees F (4.4 degrees C), suits of six millimeter thickness are available. Usually the neoprene in the torso is thicker than the neoprene in the arms and legs, allowing the surfer to retain heat around the body's core while still allowing flexible material suitable for paddling and kicking.

If the water is cold enough, surfers wear wetsuits to help them keep warm. The wetsuit is made of foam that acts as a barrier between the surfer and the cold water.

Wet suits come in different styles, including full-length and shorts, sleeveless, and other variations. Many surfers wear a rash vest under their wet suits to protect their skin from irritation. For cold water surfing, surfers wear neoprene boots, gloves, and hoods.

SURFING ACCESSORIES

In warm waters with calm waves, a surfer needs only a board and a swimsuit. But other equipment is available to make surfing safer, more convenient, and more fun. One piece of equipment that every surfer carries is surf wax. This is a hard wax, often made of paraffin or beeswax, that is rubbed on the top of the surfboard. With a good layer of wax on his board, a surfer has excellent traction and won't slip off the board.

Some deep-water surfers and stand-up paddleboard riders carry a personal locator beacon (PLB). A PLB is an emergency location device. A surfer in distress can activate the beacon. The beacon sends a distress signal to a satellite, which then translates the surfer's location and beams it back in a signal to a nearby search and rescue team. This enables search and rescue personnel to locate a surfer in danger quickly.

Many surfers use a leash so they don't lose their boards when they wipe out. A leash is a cord that is attached to the surfboard. The other end has a cuff that the surfer secures around his or her ankle.

WINDSURFING GEAR

When it comes to windsurfing boards and sails, there are hundreds of choices. Windsurfers choose their gear based on the event in which they are involved or the kind of windsurfing they want to do. Waveboards, slalom boards, and freeride boards are all different. Add the different sails and masts, and gear selection gets complicated very fast. There are three key pieces of equipment: the board, the mast, and the sail. Each windsurfing discipline uses a different combination, and the windsurfer's weight plays a big part in selection.

Beginner windsurfers use heavy boards that are wide and stable, so it is easier not to fall off. They use small sails that are easy to handle. Intermediate windsurfers add footstraps to hold their feet to the board and harnesses that attach the mast to the waist to offer better control. Beginners' sails are usually made of Dacron, which is light and inexpensive. More advanced windsurfers use sails made of Mylar, a coated Dacron that is stronger and able to withstand heavier winds.

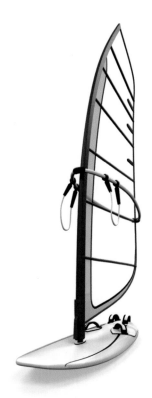

Sailboards come in many sizes, shapes and weights. The sailboard includes a board, mast, and sail. The board has straps that secure the windsurfer's feet.

Windsurfing equipment has evolved at a rapid pace. Gear that was difficult to sail with even a few years ago has improved. So it is important to use the newest gear you can when you are first learning how to windsurf.

CHAPTER FOUR

GETTING STARTED SAFELY

It's pretty awesome to watch a surfer ducking into a tube or a windsurfer jumping off of a wave and hitting a backloop. But before you can do the advanced stuff, you have to learn the basics. Almost anyone who can swim can learn to surf and wind-surf. Here are some tips to get you started and some dangers you need to be aware of.

LEARN FROM AN EXPERIENCED SURFER

One of the best ways to get started surfing is to jump right into the water with a board and the help of an expert. This could be a friend or a certified instructor. It doesn't matter, so long as you're having fun. Your introduction to surfing will probably begin on the sand, where you will learn how to move from the paddling position (on your belly) to the surfing position (on your feet). Once you master this important skill on the beach, you'll learn about some of the other aspects of surfing, like how to read waves, when to take a wave, and when to yield the right of way. Then you'll likely head out into a gentle surf to practice catching waves

32

The best way to learn to surf is to take a lesson. Beginners place their boards on the beach, where, under the watchful eye of the instructor, they practice paddling, "popping up," and holding position.

and standing up on your board. If you get the hang of it, you might stand up for one or two seconds. But keep practicing, and before you know it, you'll be surfing just like the pros!

Many kids spend a part of the summer at camp. If you want to learn to surf, you might consider a surf camp. These camps are offered everywhere in the world where there are beaches and waves. Some camps even offer kids the chance to learn from big-name pro surfers. Camps are a great way to make lifelong friends, too.

If you live near a beach where people surf, you can always find lessons or a local camp by asking the surfers. Many surf shops offer camps and lessons. This is a great way to learn all about surfing in your area and make some new friends.

Here are some of the skills that you'll learn when you take lessons or attend a camp, or even if your dad's buddy is giving you a lesson or two:

- Reading waves: Learn to pick the best waves to catch.
- Paddling: A must-have skill. After all, until you learn to stand up on a wave, you'll be paddling.
- Duck diving: When a surfer paddles out to the "line" to wait for a wave to catch, he must dive his board under oncoming waves or he'll be washed back toward shore.
- Turtle roll: Longboards are too big to duck dive, so when a wave approaches a paddling surfer, he must flip off the board and roll the board on top of him until the wave passes.
- Pop up: Every surfer needs to know how to snap up from a prone position on the board to a crouch.
- Catching waves: This is all about getting into position and timing the pop up, and it's probably the hardest part of surfing to master.
- Positioning: One key to surfing is wave position. If a surfer is high on the wave, he gets more speed. If he's low, he loses speed.
- Bottom turn: This is the first turn you'll hit once you surf down the face of the wave. You can turn back into the wave, then turn again to get your speed up again.

Once you master these beginning lessons, you'll be a full-fledged surfer!

READING WAVES

Before entering the water, surfers stand on the beach and study the waves to determine how they'll catch the best waves once they're out in the surf. They look at the angles and slopes of the waves, as well as the direction in which they break. They also judge the size of the waves, and they time the intervals between the waves. With knowledge about the conditions, surfers can predict what direction to point their surfboards when they catch a wave in order to get the best ride.

The key to good surfing is to catch waves before they close. So the surfer has to determine if the waves break to the left or right. To do this, surfers look at the skyline and the wave's angle. They identify the highest point of the wave, which is usually where the wave breaks first, splitting the wave into a left side and a right side. The side with the steepest slope is the direction of the break, and that's the direction in which they should ride the wave.

When they head out to the surf line, they'll know where to wait for waves, and they'll know which direction to paddle when it's their turn to catch a wave.

DANGERS AND SAFETY

For the most part, surfing is as safe as swimming in the ocean. Surfers are subject to the same hazards as most people who visit the beach. But because surfers play in deeper water than the typical swimmers, and because that water can be rougher than the water near the shore, surfers need to be more aware.

The biggest danger is drowning. Surfers, especially those surfing the big waves, are always in danger of "hold-downs." A hold-down happens when a surfer wipes out and is held underwater by a wave or a series of waves. The immense weight and power of a wave is too much for the surfer to swim through. A surfer also can get knocked into the seabed. Even sand is hard when a giant wave is smashing you into it. In some tropical beaches, coral reefs cover the seabed. These are sharp as razors. They cut a surfer's flesh, and the little bits left in the surfer's skin can get infected weeks later.

Another danger is riptides. A riptide is a strong current that carries water away from the shore. It also carries anything floating in the water, too, including surfers. While riptides don't pull surfers and swimmers underwater, they carry them

A surfer falls from his board. Wipeouts are a big part of surfing and are a big reason why the sport is so popular among spectators.

away from the shore. In most cases, an experienced swimmer can easily deal with a riptide. He just floats out with it, gently swimming parallel to the beach until he either moves out of the current or the current weakens. Once he is clear of the current, he can swim toward shore and catch waves into the beach.

The last big danger is marine life. The kind of marine life that can ruin a surfer's day depends on the location of the beach. Sharks, seals, sea snakes, urchins, jellyfish, and stingrays can all be hazardous. Most of the time these animals want nothing to do with surfers. But anytime man and beast share a space, there is potential for an attack. While sharks and seals have big bites, the other marine life in the list are poisonous enough to cause severe injury or death. So surfers avoid marine life whenever possible.

The best way to stay safe in the surf is to be a strong swimmer in excellent physical condition. It also helps to have enough confidence to remain calm during any situation. When some people might panic, get short of breath, and make bad decisions, experienced swimmers will remain calm and be smart.

LEARNING TO WINDSURF

Windsurfing is known as a sport that is hard to learn. As with surfing, the best way to get started with windsurfing is to take lessons. The great thing about windsurfing is that you don't have to be on a coast to learn. You can learn on a lake or even a large pond.

The beginning windsurfer learns the basics of sailing and surfing and combines them. Lessons begin with a review of the gear: the board, the mast, the sail, and the rigging. Next comes instruction on getting up on the board and uphauling the sail. Basic positions are covered, as are steering and turning.

Windsurfing is different from surfing in that it follows the rules of sailing. The windsurf board is considered a boat, and the

Because windsurfing is a combination of sailing and surfing, it can be challenging to learn. Here an instructor at a windsurfing camp shows a new windsurfer how to pull up the sail.

beginning windsurfer must learn when to give way to other boats and windsurfers. Windsurfing safety is as important as surfing safety. However, windsurfing is slightly less dangerous because the conditions are calmer and participants must wear life vests.

WHAT ARE YOU WAITING FOR?

Surfing and windsurfing are exciting sports for people of all ages. They are safe ways to enjoy action in the great outdoors. The younger you start, the sooner you'll be on your way. With the proper training and instruction, anyone who is reasonably fit and a pretty good swimmer will enjoy learning how to shred waves and sail with the wind. So get out there!

GLOSSARY

blank The block of foam from which a surfboard is carved.

bottom turn The first turn at the bottom of a wave.

break The area where the waves break just off the beach.

close When or where a wave breaks.

cutback A turn cutting back toward the wave.

freeride A category of sailboard used for sailing back and forth as fast and comfortably as possible.

gnarliest The most gnarly; the most difficult, dangerous, or challenging.

lineup The area where the waves begin to break, usually where surfers are positioned to catch waves.

mast The long pole used to hold the sail to the board.

pop up Moving from lying down on a surfboard to standing in a crouch in a single motion.

riptide A strong, narrow current that carries water away from the shore.

slalom A high-speed windsurfing race either in a figure-eight or around markers.

tube Where the wave is hollow as it is breaking, almost enclosing the surfer. Also called a barrel.

uphauling When the windsurfer pulls the rope attached to the sail to pull the sail out of the water.

wipe out To fall off of a surfboard.

Endless Summer Surf Camp
P.O. Box 414
San Clemente, CA 92674
(949) 498-7862
Website: http://www.endlesssummersurfcamp.com
The Endless Summer Surf Camp features a variety of surf camps
    to suit the needs of almost everyone. There are day camps and
    overnight camps for adults and kids.

International Funboard Class Association
Mengham Cottage, Mengham Lane
Hayling Island,
Hampshire PO11 9JX
England
++ 4423 9246 8831
Website: http://www.ifca.internationalwindsurfing.com
The IFCA is the governing body of international windsurfing competition
    for the Aloha, Formula, Funboard, and Raceboard classes.

International Surfing Association
5580 La Jolla Boulevard, #145
La Jolla, CA 92037
(858) 551-8580
Website: http://www.isasurf.org
The International Surfing Association (ISA) is recognized by the
    International Olympic Committee (IOC) as the world governing
    authority for surfing, stand-up paddle (SUP) surfing and racing, and
    all other wave riding activities.

National Scholastic Surfing Association
P.O. Box 495

Huntington Beach, CA 92648

(714) 906-7423

Website: http://www.nssa.org

The NSSA is a nonprofit organization that promotes the qualities of discipline and competitive excellence while supporting the merits of academic achievement to young surfers. The NSSA strives to provide a fun surfing experience for all of its members.

Surfing America, Inc.

555 N. El Camino Real

Suite A126

San Clemente, CA 92672

(949) 391-1010

Website: http://www.surfingamerica.org

As the official ISA-recognized national governing body for the sport of surfing in the United States, Surfing America is responsible for holding the USA Surfing Championships event each year and for selecting the official USA Surf Team to compete internationally.

Surfing Association of Nova Scotia (SANS)

49 Hawthorne Street

Dartmouth, NS B2Y 2Y7

Canada

(902) 478-1146

Website: http://www.surfns.com

Established in 1987, SANS is a community-based nonprofit organization dedicated to building an inclusive, fun, and respectful surf community; supporting recreational and amateur surfing; and fostering coastal stewardship.

U.S. Windsurfing Association
510 Cascade Street
Suite 100
Hood River, OR 97031
(877) 386-8708
Website: http://www.uswindsurfing.org
U.S. Windsurfing is a member-based organization that ensures
the growth of recreational and competitive windsurfing in the
United States. Its mission is accomplished via the provision of
products, services, and marketing activities that are designed to
meet the needs of all its member groups.

WEBSITES

Because of the changing nature of Internet links, Rosen Publishing has
developed an online list of websites related to the subject of this book.
This site is updated regularly. Please use this link to access the list:

http://www.rosenlinks.com/STTE/Surf

FOR FURTHER READING

Booth, Douglas. *Surfing: The Ultimate Guide.* San Francisco, CA: Greenwood, 2011.

Dugan, Christine. *Hang Ten! Surf.* Huntington Beach, CA: Teacher Created Materials, 2013.

Hamilton, S. L. *Surfing.* Edina, MN: ABDO, 2010.

Mason, Paul. *Surfing: The World's Most Fantastic Surf Spots and Techniques.* Mankato, MN: Capstone Press, 2011.

McCloud, Andrea. *The Girl's Guide to Surfing.* San Francisco, CA: Chronicle Books, 2011.

Robison, John. *Surfing Illustrated: A Visual Guide to Wave Riding.* Camden, ME: International Marine/Ragged Mountain Press, 2010.

BIBLIOGRAPHY

Encyclopedia of Surfing. "Kahanamoku, Duke." Retrieved October 5, 2014 (http://encyclopediaofsurfing.com/entries/kahanamoku-duke).

Extreme Horizon. "Beginners Guide to Essential Surfing Equipment." Retrieved October 11, 2014 (http://www.extremehorizon.com/surf-shop/surfing_equipment.html).

Hawaiian Encyclopedia. "The History of Surfing." Retrieved October 2, 2014 (http://www.hawaiianencyclopedia.com/the-history-of-surfing.asp).

How Products Are Made. "Surfboard." Retrieved October 11, 2014 (http://www.madehow.com/Volume-2/Surfboard.html).

Kampion, Drew. *Stoked! A History of Surf Culture*. Layton, UT : Gibbs Smith Publisher, 2003.

Marcus, Ben. "From Polynesia, with Love." Retrieved October 2, 2014 (http://www.surfingforlife.com/history.html).

Northeast Surfing. "History of Surfing." Retrieved October 2, 2014 (http://northeastsurfing.com/education/history).

Statistic Brain. "Surfing Statistics." Retrieved October 11, 2014 (http://www.statisticbrain.com/surfing-statistics).

Washaw, Matt. *The History of Surfing*. San Francisco, CA: Chronicle Books, 2010.

Westwick, Peter, and Peter Neushul. *The World in the Curl: An Unconventional History of Surfing*. New York, NY: Crown, 2013.

INDEX

ABOUT THE AUTHOR

J. Poolos has been an avid surfer since he first paddled out to the break off the coast of Northern California in 1993. He has written numerous young adult nonfiction books on topics that include events of historical significance and biographies of sports heroes.

PHOTO CREDITS

Cover, p. 4 (surfer), p. 5 EpicStockMedia/Shutterstock.com; cover, pp. 1, 3, 6, 15, 24, 32 (seascape) Willyam Bradberry/Shutterstock.com; p. 7 Universal History Archive/UIG/Getty Images; p. 8 Dennis Macdonald/Photolibrary/Getty Images; p. 11 Michael Ochs Archives/Getty Images; p. 13 © AP Images; pp. 16–17 Ed Sloane/ASP/Getty Images; pp. 18–19 Sacramento Bee/Tribune News Service/Getty Images; p. 20 Ezra Shaw/Getty Images; p. 22 Purestock/Thinkstock; p. 25 Bloomberg/Getty Images; pp. 26–27 JJDIGITAL/Shutterstock.com; p. 29 Anthony Ong/Digital Vision/Thinkstock; p. 31 Nerthuz/Shutterstock.com; p. 33 Erik Snyder/Digital Vision/Thinkstock; pp. 36–37 jarvis gray/Shutterstock.com; p. 39 Portland Press Herald/Getty Images; cover and interior pages graphics SkillUp/Shutterstock.com, Sfio Cracho/Shutterstock.com, saicle/Shutterstock.com, Frank Rohde/Shutterstock.com, Thomas Bethge/Shutterstock.com, nortivision/Shutterstock.com, PinkPueblo/Shutterstock.com.

Designer: Michael Moy; Editor: Christine Poolos